Mastering Ethereum:

The Ultimate Guide for Beginners to Understanding Ethereum Technology, Ethereum Investing, Ethereum Mining and Other Cryptocurrencies.

Anthony Tu

For more information, go to

www.wonpublications.com

Table of Contents

About the Author

Anthony Tu (also known as Anthony Tuanga) is a computer scientist, author and a cryptocurrency investor. He has been working in the field of computer science for the last 10 years and completed his degree at Harvard University. He came across cryptocurrencies early in 2011 and fell in love with the technology.

He is a large investor in cryptocurrencies such as Bitcoin, Ethereum and continues to share his vast knowledge in the space.

Outside of work, he is a family man. He loves to spend time with his beautiful wife and son.

Introduction

I want to thank you for choosing and purchasing this book, *'Mastering Ethereum: The Ultimate Guide for Beginners to Understanding Ethereum Technology, Ethereum Investing, Ethereum Mining and Other Cryptocurrencies."* In this book you'll find everything you need to know about Ethereum, from the history of Ethereum, to the nitty gritty side of Ethereum Mining. This book will be your ultimate guide and something you can refer to now, and also in the future. As a BONUS, not only is this book about the essentials of Ethereum, information about other Cryptocurrencies will be added for your benefit.

If you're new to Cryptocurrencies, you may be wondering what on earth is the term 'Ethereum'? I myself was curious too. I wondered if it was some sort of new sci-fi movie that was released or an extension of the never ending Transformers saga. In some ways it could be, but that we will have to wait. In this present day, Ethereum is a new age revolution, being the second biggest cryptocurrency after Bitcoin. It has made headlines all around the world being the leader in alternative coins, allowing itself to explode in value in 2017. If you're familiar with cryptocurrencies, the term 'Ethereum', is just another text book, day-to-day word we all use. I myself started investing into cryptocurrencies with Ethereum, and if you've read my previous book, 'Mastering Bitcoin', you'd know I started investing because of my friend. Not only did he make an outstanding 400% return on his investment, he told me his next investment project was Ethereum. I was curious to know what this was and I studied everything I could about Ethereum, and here we are.

I know you are excited to learn about Ethereum, and we'll get started in a second. Again, I'd like to thank you for choosing this book. I have comprised everything I know about Ethereum in my years of experience, and I know you'll enjoy this book. This is the beginning of your cryptocurrency adventure and I hope you're as excited as I am.

At the end of this book, you'll be given a FREE step-by-step course so that you can start investing in Bitcoin today!

Let's get started!

For easy understanding, we will start from the very beginning of bitcoins and cryptocurrencies.

Chapter 1: Basics of Cryptocurrency

Cryptocurrency is the name given to any digital currency that is deemed secure because of cryptography — or a particular kind of encryption method that's perfect for the whole blockchain process. What's amazing about cryptocurrencies is that no central authorities govern them. They are organic and are a perfect system on their own. The government or anyone not involved in Blockchain cannot manipulate them in any way— keeping your funds always in check. In fact, it is virtually impossible for any governing body to track down any transactions and associate it to an individual. This is what makes cryptocurrencies so fascinating and why some governments are highly against cryptocurrencies.

One thing about cryptocurrency transactions is that they might be used for illicit activities — such as tax evasion or even money laundering. Prior to larger adoption in 2017, particularly the early years, there has been a lot of controversy about the uses of cryptocurrencies, that it is only used for activity done on dark web, including drug dealings.

This is different in 2017 where there has been a larger acceptance of cryptocurrencies, with some banks incorporating the Blockchain technology and various companies accepting cryptocurrencies as a form of payment. The main argument towards cryptocurrencies is the ability for parties to easily send and accept funds from each other, even in cryptocurrency form, and only with minimal transaction fees. There are also many other uses for cryptocurrency, including crowdfunding and online voting. After all, people find it easier to spend online currencies instead of real ones— they don't cause too much hassle either.

Cryptocurrency is money created by the use of encryption techniques of advanced computer programming. These same techniques are used to carry out and verify the transfer of funds. Cryptocurrencies are independent of central banks and are decentralized. This means that parties can send and receive funds directly towards each other without a middleman. For most people, sending money is a hassle, particularly when you want to send money abroad. If you're transferring money between local banks, it could potentially take days for the banks to clear and verify the transactions to be made. When sending abroad, this is a different case; in certain situations this could take more than a week, let alone the fees of processing the transactions. Some major companies like Western Union allow faster transactions, but it comes at a cost, the fees.

The implications of cryptocurrency are so great that some central banks have attempted to involve themselves in the technology, with some attempting to issue their own cryptocurrencies. However, the currency they produce is not officially considered cryptocurrency as they can only develop centralized money. The idea behind decentralization is to allow the open market to influence the power. With centralization, all the power and control is with the centralized body, the central banks, meaning that you and I have no say in how much money is created or what it's worth. In this sense, the Federal Reserve can manipulate the value of traditional currencies (i.e US Dollar) via printing more money and there's nothing we can do. The proponents of cryptocurrency are very keen on keeping the "true" digital currency decentralized and because of this, cryptocurrencies have seen to be very favorable. Because of the unique nature of cryptocurrencies, is it actually deflationary, as time goes on, the value of most cryptocurrencies will go higher.

Rise of Cryptocurrency

Cryptocurrencies, such as Bitcoin, Ethereum, Litecoin and others, have had a lot of publicity, particularly in 2017. This is primarily due to the large exposure given by the news, social media and financial institutions. As the levels of financial/digital literacy of the general population have increased, cryptocurrency acceptance has also made leaps in purchasing power. In 2010, a Bitcoin investor, known as Laslo, claimed to have purchased two pizzas for roughly 10,000 Bitcoins. It was considered the first instance where a cryptocurrency was used to make a purchase. At the time, Bitcoins were virtually worthless. As of November 2017, Bitcoin is valued higher than gold, with one-coin worth nearly $10,000!

At first, most were very skeptical of Bitcoin and its technology, seeing it as a form of counterfeit or a device of criminals. This was particularly so when it was publicized as the means of trade on the 'Silk Road,' a part of the dark Internet where all sorts of unsavory behavior were rampant.

However, there is now an increasing involvement of legitimate business and government with cryptocurrency. New applications and even ATM's are incorporated to allow cryptocurrency transactions to occur. As a consequence, the market capitalization of all cryptocurrencies is more than $250,000,000,000!

By Mid 2017, we have seen a rise in cryptocurrencies, revealing more than 1000 cryptocurrencies. Most people have heard of Bitcoin, especially since recent ransomware attacks have demanded payment in Bitcoins. The benefit to criminals of this is that any such payment by a victim would be untraceable.

If the website for coinmarketcap is checked, it will be seen that there is a small graph beside the type of cryptocurrency, each showing the movement of the currency in the last week, as well as the percentage change in the last 24 hours. It will be seen that there is a significant disparity in the values of the various cryptocurrencies with one Bitcoin being worth nearly $10,000 and a total market capitalization of more than $150,000,000,000. Another cryptocurrency called Bytecoin was worth less than one cent although the total capitalization of Bytecoins was more than $200,000,000. Some cryptocurrencies have small capitalizations. An example is MikeTheMug cryptocurrency with a capitalization of approximately $1000!

Just reading this, you may be wondering how a coin like 'MikeTheMug' can be taken seriously, and with all due respect for MikeTheMug, it is actually easier than most people think to create and issue a coin, which makes some individuals quite skeptical about cryptocurrencies.

Though there are a lot of valid and exciting potential projects within cryptocurrencies, it should be noted there are also a lot of 'joke' coins with no actual fundamental value. A good example is Dogecoin that I myself do find quite hysterical, however, the coin itself serves no real purpose aside from representing the patriotism that society has created through hysterical memes and the Internet. To put that in perspective, Dogecoin has a market cap of more than $200,000,000, based on a meme of a dog.

We will have more to say about the quality and worth of cryptocurrencies later.

Cryptocurrency as Money

The people involved in cryptocurrency call the currencies we use, in everyday life, 'fiat', or 'fiat currency' Despite the word 'currency' in the word cryptocurrency, there are greater similarities between cryptocurrencies and stocks than cryptocurrencies and fiat currencies. A purchase of some cryptocurrency is similarly a purchase of a technology stock, an entry in a digital ledger called a blockchain, and a part of the digital network for that cryptocurrency. Buying cryptocurrencies is similarly to stock purchasing because each 'cryptocurrency' represents a different project. When you purchase these cryptocurrencies, you're buying a share within the project. An example of which is Ethereum or Ether. Having Ether allows the investor to participate in voting within the Ethereum network.

Cryptocurrency is a means of exchange that uses cryptography so that transactions are secure. They are used to exercise control over the manufacture of further units of the currency. Cryptocurrencies are a type of what is called alternative currencies; different from traditional currencies such as everyone is familiar with, the US Dollar, the Euro, the British Pound, etc.

Due to their frequent and great fluctuations in value, one of the two fundamentals of money, namely "a store of value" is lacking. Within any new markets, there are large fluctuations in the prices of the assets. But as the market begins to grow over time, you will see price stability as well as more institutional and commercial uses. A good example is the stock market within periods of recessions, where uncertainty generally leads to large fluctuations in prices. However, most of the time, the prices of the large capitalization companies in the stock market are fairly stable. Within the cryptocurrency market, Bitcoin is starting to unfold as the most stable cryptocurrency.

Quite ironically, Bitcoin was initially released to allow decentralized peer-to-peer transactions to take place, but because of the explosive popularity of Bitcoin in recent years,

Bitcoin has seen to become more of a store value due to ridiculous costs to transfer Bitcoin in between wallets. A lot of individuals see Bitcoin as the gold standard within the cryptocurrency world, and much like gold is to be held, a lot of investors choose to hold Bitcoin within the cryptocurrency market. Some digital currencies exhibit the behavior of countries having significant inflation in that value is not retained.

Chapter 2: History of Ethereum

A Brief History on Ethereum

Ethereum was originally proposed in late 2013 with the initial release of its white paper by Russian-born Canadian, Vitalik Buterin. Buterin was not satisfied with the nature of Bitcoin. It would be too complex to change and this formed his desire to create a new platform instead, named Ethereum. During prior release, in 2014, there was an online sale that pushed the Ethereum coin into the market, however it wasn't until mid 2015, roughly one and half years later after the initial release of the white paper, when the Ethereum project officially went live and running. Due the dozens, if not hundreds of developers, engineers and scientists that were working on the project, Ethereum exceeded expectations, resulting in a rapid expansion. This allowed Ethereum to release projects frequently and has allowed Ethereum to become the second biggest cryptocurrency today (as of October 2017)

What is a Cryptocurrency?

Cryptocurrency is a coined terminology that primarily deals with a bit of encrypted text that represents a value in a market. The way a cryptocurrency normally works is that you have a username (known as an address) that represents your identity in the cryptocurrency network and you also have a small bit of encrypted text that comes after your username that represents the actual coin that is in your possession. Whenever you trade that coin, the username is switched but the encrypted text stays the same. Since the text is encrypted with a very powerful encryption system, this makes the coin very rare and thus creates value in the coin.

What does it mean to be Decentralized?

To understand this, let's go ahead and go over how money has actually evolved over time. In the beginning, it was not even money that allowed us to exchange things. During the beginning of civilization, we primarily traded items rather than money and this was because not a lot of people had the same resource. However, as populations expanded and resource manipulation expanded, those resources became duplicative and the market had the problem of mismatch in product demands. This essentially was a case where somebody had something that was similar to a lamb or a fruit and they tried to trade it to somebody who had plenty of lambs or fruits. This created a massive problem due to the fact that if you couldn't trade for the items that you needed then you would easily just spiral down into what would essentially be stone-age poverty. Then someone had the bright idea to take items and turn that into gold. Gold represented a standard and it also represented the worth of an item. The rarity of gold allowed it to be utilized as the very first form of coin monetization. Having said that, gold actually wasn't the first because they didn't really know how to transform gold just yet and so the very first one was copper because of how common it was. People were able to trade this this type of currency whenever they wanted to but as copper became less and less rare, its' value begin to drop drastically and so this is when silver came into the picture. The same thing happened to silver until gold came into the picture. The same thing happened to gold and nothing changed.

Essentially, we are all kept agreeing on the gold value. Gold has been the primary monetary value in the marketplace for the past 2000 years until somebody had the bright idea to change physical, rare metals into paper representation of those metals. This is what we know as the gold standard. This meant that for every dollar, there was a specific dollar amount that would equal a specific gold amount. While I may be talking about dollars, this was the representation of most of the money in the world. The problem is that money is limited and if you really want to make a good amount of money, you can't really make that money if someone has all that money in the first place. Establishing a gold standard basically put a cap limit on how much a person can progress. Therefore, the gold standard was changed into what we know as Fiat money. Fiat money is known as a type of money that is symbolic in nature. You put your worth on the dollar bill. If no one actually saw value in the dollar bill because it is Fiat money, the dollar bill would no longer be worth anything. This has been the standard for the past hundred years.

Then in 2009, we came out with cryptocurrency. However, there's a special component of Fiat money that you need to understand before we delve into cryptocurrency. You see, for the dollar, the money is actually printed by one organization that is controlled by a private bank known as the Federal Reserve. This private bank chooses how much to print each year so that money continues to be a useful item in our society. Over time, this printed amount becomes unmanageable in cases that you can see such as Greece falling or Japan falling. Essentially, there is so much paper money in the works that it becomes pennies rather than dollars and so no one wants to work with it. The only way that anyone has saved themselves from these pennies is to go to a new Fiat money. For the longest time the American dollar has held the gold standard when it comes to Fiat money. Everybody thought it would be a good idea to place their trust in America because of how big and powerful it was in the financial and military realm. The problem is that America as a whole is a good country but the corporations that control the vast majority of the wealth are generally not that intelligent. During 2008, we suffered the biggest recession that we've seen since the Great Depression. The American dollar has been losing value ever since and since the biggest loaner to America is China, China doesn't want to be caught in a situation where the debtor cannot pay his debt. This brings us to cryptocurrency, which is a new form of Fiat money but at a finite amount. You see, there is no one that can tell the Bitcoin or the Ethereum to print more. Bitcoin and Ethereum simply print as much as they are programmed to print and they don't even print it, they just digitally create the numbers in the monetary spheres that is Bitcoin and Ethereum . Decentralization means that there is no one company that controls the vast majority of how Bitcoin or Ethereum is produced and so since there is no one controlling this massive cryptocurrency, there is no central governing body. Everybody checks everybody and it is a mixture of the days when we used to trade each other with actual items and Fiat money. For many, this is seen as the evolution of money.

What is an Altcoin?

Normally when somebody refers to an Altcoin they are actually referring to an alternative cryptocurrency coin that is not Bitcoin. Bitcoin represents the beginning of the cryptocurrency trend and so it's usually referred to as the original cryptocurrency coin but the truth is the Bitcoin really isn't the first cryptocurrency, it's just the first cryptocurrency coin that became popular. Alternative cryptocurrency represents a market of cryptocurrencies rather than a specific individual cryptocurrency. People refer to them as alternative cryptocurrency coins otherwise known as Altcoins simply because it came after Bitcoin.

Ethereum vs. Ethereum Classic

The Ethereum blockchain is written in C++, Go, and Rust, which are all very powerful and very quick languages. The best part is that it was written for x86 systems and ARM platforms so it will not be going away for a long time. However, the system was closed off in its own little environment for a very long time and it was not public, and so in 2015, around 12 million coins flooded the market for sales, and ever since then it's been a crazy ride. Now, Ethereum has experienced some problems and this has resulted in two different Ethereum, Ethereum and Ethereum Classic. You might be wondering where in the world do Ethereum and Ethereum classic come from and how do they differentiate. Well, there was a project called the DAO, which was a way of formalizing contracts as a way of transactions in businesses. The problem is that because of security issues, this project failed and the result of this issue actually ended up creating a divergent point between the two different cryptocurrencies. This created a 'hardfork' which is essentially a split in the Blockchain, resulting in the two Ethereum today. So they are technically both Ethereum but Ethereum Classic follows an older pattern while the Ethereum you know today has a little bit more security add to do it.

Chapter 3: How Cryptocurrency Works?

What is an Ether Blockchain

A blockchain is known as the Ledger of whatever cryptocurrency that you're talking about because it keeps all of the records of all the transactions that have ever happened as well as all of the current coins in rotation. This is a linked list of hashed pointers that keep a timestamp of the current transaction along with the transaction data required to make the transaction. This blockchain is then distributed amongst everyone in the cryptocurrency network so that they can double-check any transaction that is currently taking place. An 'Ether' is simply the token of the Ethereum blockchain. The Ether token is used within this network to run operations, much like money in day-to-day society, Ether is essentially money of the Ethereum network. It is also known as 'ETH' in cryptocurrency markets.

Free Beginnings

When a cryptocurrency first lands on the market, it's usually free and this is because the only usual way to get it around to people is to make it free. People are not going to simply invest their time and money in something that's literally worth nothing. However, once people actually own it and they begin to play around with it, these currencies begin to gain attraction and therefore gain value. However, we see a very clear trend with most cryptocurrencies that they start out free so that people can test them and to see how reliable they are and then the market begins to accept it. This actually happened with Bitcoin where a vast majority of the beginning users received free Bitcoins as a result of doing something that the developers of Bitcoin wanted them to do. The actual value of Bitcoin didn't rise until much later in the Bitcoin life cycle as it stands right now.

Market Rarity Equals Value

However, once the market actually gets the coins, the value of that coin begins to rise because people have it and other people don't. This is true about every type of currency that has ever existed. Gold was really something that only the rich had during the medieval times simply because of how rare the gold was while the everyday peasant had a copper coin that they could utilize in the markets. Once the coin got onto the market, the value of the coin began to increase but the coins value is based on how rare the coin actually is so if you can begin to control the rarity of the coin then you can actually control the value of the coin itself. However, cryptocurrencies provide a different form of rarity. You see, previous monetization values such as gold and copper became rare because their existence was rare. Cryptocurrency becomes rare because the more people that join in the game of mining cryptocurrency the harder it is to mine those cryptocurrencies. Therefore, you need more and more power in order to get those cryptocurrencies and only those with the most amount of power get the most amount of cryptocurrencies. This process increases the rarity of the cryptocurrency and this in turn raises the value of the cryptocurrency. You can think of this process much like *deflation*, the less there is, the rarer it is.

Releasing Coins Decreases Value

Every time coins are released into the market, the value of those coins temporarily goes down because the coins represented a certain value before those coins got released and then the value goes down because there's more coins in the market. This is a very temporary bend in the value of the coin because once the coins have been released into the market, then everyone has to mine for more coins out of more difficult rates and this is what increases the overall value of the cryptocurrency. You can think of this process much like *inflation*, the more there is, the less rare it is.

Proof of Work Increases Market Value

As I already mentioned before, the market value of cryptocurrency is based on how difficult it is to mine for these coins. This is done by the concept of proof of work. Previously, digital currencies had no ways of proving that they were the original copy simply because you were capable of copying and pasting all sorts of documents because they're digital. This was known as the double spending law but if you have a ledger that keeps all of the transactions that have happened including the mining of new currencies, then you have the ability to stop double spending. Essentially, you have the market that is using those currencies, and those mining for currencies. The miners check for the validations of those transactions so that if a currency tries to double spend, the market that actually uses that currency double-checks who actually has that currency and if the person who currently has the currency is not the person that is trading over the currency, the market rejects the transaction. This is known as the proof-of-work concept and it's also how cryptocurrency mining actually occurs. You are simply checking to make sure that everybody is making appropriate transactions in the network and when the network wants to make a transaction check, it sends out the check amongst everyone in the network and the first one to figure it out gets a small package of coins but the network shares those coins amongst all the computers that served to figure out the encryption puzzle to check if the appropriate transaction took place. We know this as the blockchain. The Ethereum platform has been based off of the same proof-of-work concept that Bitcoin was based off but now they are attempting to make the move to proof of stake, which allows for the use of virtual mining.

To Come: Proof of Stake

The problem with proof of work is that it consumes massive amounts of energy, as shown when we dive into actually mining coins ourselves later on in this book. Eventually, they will reach a point where there are no more Bitcoins to provide the people who are known as cryptocurrency miners with the rewards they currently treasure. At that time, the value of Bitcoin is pretty much determined by the transaction fees that go along with any transactions on the Bitcoin Network. Since this doesn't really require the Goliath sized workload of the cryptocurrency Farms that are out there, there's no real reason for miners to not just accept every transaction fee that any person creates. This means that the transaction fee will go down and the lack of money making possibilities will cause miners to simply disappear from the network. On the other hand, Ethereum provides a different way of earning these coins and that is to say that you have a certain amount of stake inside of Ethereum. Essentially, the miners of Ethereum will also run out of coins to mine but in order to reward miners of Ethereum, those that have the most amount of coins can then mine the most amount of coins. In other words, if you managed to obtain 2% of all the Ethereum that's on the network then you are also allowed to mine 2% of all the Ethereum on the network. This allows individuals to continuously build up their resources without sacrificing the hardware that Bitcoin chomps on. Instead, it's about who can perform the most amount of transactions now but, to make it fair, the system randomizes the choice of who gets to mine. This is because the calculation for how many Ethereum coins an individual has is a very easy calculation for the network to provide as a way of validation. The network keeps track of how many coins a certain account has and if you have the same amount of coins as listed in the account, it serves as a validation but if you have less you get less of a reward. It's a very easy way of calculating for the purpose of validation but there are quite a few problems with it and there may be more problems to come so since the actual concept hasn't been implemented in Ethereum just yet, we will let the future decide what problems will come of this.

Chapter 4: Smart Contracts

What is a Smart Contract?

All right, so the coolest thing about Ethereum is the ability to utilize smart contracts but a lot of people get confused between a regular contract and a smart contract. However, let's talk about this in the form of automobiles because a lot of people know how to purchase an automobile and if you're reading this book, the odds that you've purchased an automobile is pretty high. In this process, you first go to a notable dealership or used car salesman and you inspect the product beforehand, then you talk it out and determine which is the best price for you before you go to the bank and request money out of your bank. Your bank then utilizes a safety system known as a certified check or a direct check that the bank personally takes responsibility for and then provides you that money. This money is then taken to the dealership where the individual who is selling the car now begins the process of giving you the car. Both you and the dealership or the used cars salesman is in a long drawn-out process of filling out information so that all of the information can be deposited to the DMV. This DMV serves as a giant file bucket to verify who owns what cars and when they obtained them. Once the DMV approves your car, you then have to register your car to the DMV so that they can up keep the cost of holding those files. Meanwhile, you have to take the car home and apply things like insurance and that is the end of the chain for buying a car. If you notice, this process was actually slowed down due to two major things. The first thing is that your bank needed to give you a way to secure the amount of money that is on a check because a personal check could be bounced and the bank knows that the person selling you the car needs a check that is the value that they are wanting. Therefore, they created the system called a secure check, which allows the person selling the item to rely on the bank's reputation rather than the individual buying the car to back the money up. Then, a file is needed to be kept so that the dealership couldn't just say "oh he never bought that car" and just take the car back even though he got the money. He could easily say that the money was just given to him out of being a nice stranger although I highly doubt that that is something that would happen. However, there is still that possibility so what the DMV needs to do is it needs to register who actually owns the car, when they bought it and keep all the different details on the car. These two processes took a system that would normally take maybe a day to complete and turned it into nearly a week or more depending on how difficult your system that you have to deal with is.

That was a standard contract and this new contract, otherwise known as a smart contract, is different and better. The smart contract is built on to the blockchain that makes Ethereum worth investing and why it's a cryptocurrency. This automatically makes the contract trustworthy. The cryptocurrency itself is a trusted form of money and you can't just make up the amount of money that you have in cryptocurrency so the money is its own secure check. Since the information on the car could easily be uploaded to the blockchain for further information of who owned the car and the details of the car, you no longer need the DMV. Essentially, you would go and look at a car to where you would want to buy it and you would be able to buy it on the spot whether it is online or offline. You see, in this chain you would go find the car that you wanted that was attached to the blockchain and then you would transfer the Ethereum from your account into the blockchain and if it met the amount that the dealer was asking for then the car would be given to you.

Since the money is trusted and the information in the blockchain is trusted, there is no need for these middlemen called the bank and the DMV. The best part about this is the reason why most cars are not sold online is due to the fact that you have to deal with your local DMV and bank and so most places build a giant shop and take up land just because we have to deal with these middlemen. Instead of dealing with these organizations, we can bring the car industry into the online space and we can begin exchanging these cars like the products that we should have been exchanging them long before we started exchanging things like toothpaste on Amazon and voltmeters on eBay. This is the power of a smart contract and this is the difference between a smart contract and a regular contract.

The First Design

The first design or rather the first concept of a smart contract actually developed in 1996 by Nick's Szabo. The idea that he created was actually that the smart contract would be utilized for a much wider spectrum that could be defined with very specific boundaries created by logic and would eventually be enforced through the protocols created by cryptography. The problem is that these smart contracts were really the idea of how you could further the process of creating the computations needed in order to maintain the blockchain itself. The actual idea as we know of it right now is not one where individuals are capable of making online transactions that remove middlemen but more of the idea of how to maintain the validity of a blockchain. The first popular form of a smart contract was actually known as DAO and this was for a venture capital funding campaign that was currently running on Ethereum but then the ironic part about this is that the platform was hacked and all the Ethereum was drained in literally less than a month.

The Implementations that Followed

While Ethereum is the most widely used cryptocurrency when it comes to Smart contracts, there are actually others that have utilized this technology. For instance, RootStock is a powerful platform that is derived off of the Bitcoin blockchain that acts as a smart contract platform but this technology, of course, works with Ethereum as well. Then you have cryptocurrencies like Burstcoin and Qora, which utilize the notion of automated transactions but these are not the general purpose ideas that we think of whenever we think of smart contracts with Ethereum.

The Flaws in Smart Contracts

Now as much as smart contracts seem like they are the cars of tomorrow, they are built off of code and code usually has bugs in it. If the actual code itself doesn't have bugs in it then the virtual machine that runs it has bugs, the compiler itself may have bugs, the network blockchain can be DDOSed into submitting to a certain will, the bugs (on the network, if they are found) will be slow to repair, and there are a lot of problems with smart contracts. A lot of people like to act like this is the Holy Grail of all contracts but due to the flaws of programmatic error, we have so many bugs that could happen that it is actually somewhat difficult to fully trust a smart contract. Until the system is designed so that it is nearly agreed to be perfect, smart contracts are not likely to enter any markets where government backing or medical industry guarantees are capable of carrying out those guarantees without fear of the system being the problem.

What do Gas and Ether mean in the Ethereum Environment?

Whenever there is a transaction on the Ethereum environment, there has to be an operational task that is meant to validate and verify both sides of the exchanging parties currencies so that the Ethereum network avoids the double spending problem. As odd as it may seem, you actually spend Ether in the Ethereum environment and you get Ether coins in exchange for mining them. However, if you were to transfer them to a person then you would be charged a Gas fee (Gas is the internal pricing for running a transaction or contract in the Ethereum network). Gas fees are non-refundable to either party and the system automatically converts the Ether into Gas in order to pay for the fee for the operational costs it took to run the transaction. This Gas is then distributed amongst the Ethereum network as rewards for continuously perpetuating the Ethereum network. This is very different from Bitcoin because Bitcoin actually has a set limit on how much cryptocurrency is going to come out in the future to the point of 21 million whereas Ethereum was built with the limitation in mind and so whenever a transaction occurs, a little bit of that transaction goes back into the environment and since transactions are happening all the time a ton of Ethereum is going back into the Ethereum environment.

What is an Oracle?

Now when I said that smart contracts have the potential to remove the middlemen that we have to deal with, that isn't entirely true because smart contracts are not as capable as they're made out to be. You see, smart contracts do have the capabilities of securing data on the network so that a transaction is cleared much like the way I described. The problem is that that information has no way to actually get into the network and this is where something called an Oracle comes in. An Oracle serves as the middleman for the cryptocurrency coin and the cryptocurrency blockchain. Essentially, it allows the individuals on the network to develop an API that gives the financial individuals that want to work with smart contracts the ability to interact with this smart contract technology. Therefore, Oracles are probably one of the more annoying problems that we're going to have to deal with because the smart contracts on the network are not all that good by default. Essentially, we have to do what HTML did for the World Wide Web. The World Wide Web was originally just text based files and there were no real way to look at a web page. Essentially, the world wide web looked like a giant file system. Therefore, somebody came along and developed HTML and you see where that ended up.

What is Timestamping?

A timestamp, in the digital sense, represents the time at which something occurred and it acts as a stamp because it records that time and only that time. This is very simpler to think of if you were to think of an accountant in keeping transactions of when certain transactions occurred. The only difference between the timestamp that the accountant uses and the timestamp that the computer uses is that the computer will usually record down to the smallest possible version of time that you can possibly conceive of so as to get a very accurate description of exactly when that happened. Therefore, an accountant would say that something happened at 3:45, but a computer would say that it happened at 3, 45 minutes from 3, and 21 nanoseconds from 45 minutes. In other words it would look something like this:

3:45:0000029.As you can see, you can get far more precise transaction times and normally transactions will not happen at the exact same nanosecond so the validity of the system is very reliable. The Bitcoin currency system or rather the cryptocurrency system is not the first type of program that utilizes this timestamp because whenever you do anything with credit cards, anything with practically all the different social media applications, and even your phone application, they all use this version of timestamp because it accurately records when things happened so that they can put it in the proper order.

Chapter 5: The Potential of Ethereum

The Latency of Ethereum

The process in which Ethereum checks for the validation of transactions is actually faster than that of Bitcoin which means that there can be a lot more transactions occurring than with Bitcoin. Additionally, the Ethereum actually utilizes more nodes than Bitcoin so it is more security proof so not only is it faster in this case but it is also providing the additional benefit of being more robust in its' security.

Why Ethereum is a Long-Term Investment?

The core concepts behind these two cryptocurrencies are practically the same but the reason why Ethereum is seen as a long-term investment is primarily due to the giant corporations that have taken a look at Ethereum. The core concept of smart contracts is the reason why Ethereum is currently the long-term investment for most individuals because Bitcoin doesn't have a competing technology for this and smart contracts are a vital part of an ecosystem built off of money. In other words, the smart contract allows individuals to begin replacing jobs and increasing the validation for transactions while Bitcoin just doesn't do that. This is why Ethereum is seen as the long-term investment of these two cryptocurrencies.

The Legality of Ethereum?

The legality of Ethereum is very similar to the legality of Bitcoin but the problem with Ethereum is the smart contract itself. If these smart contracts come in to replace contracts then it removes so many jobs that it is mind-blowing. There are so many jobs that are built in place simply to validate transactions because you have the DMV, which is utilized to validate transactions with cars and sometimes tickets. You have The Mailing Service, which is utilized to validate that a package has arrived either through digital format or physical format and one person could literally do the job of this validation so instead of the one person collecting all the packages information and ensuring that it was sent out that morning, you have Ethereum just keeping track of whether the item was delivered at the door or not. You have Banks period. Banks are the ones that would literally topple over if this became the mainstream thing. Banks would actually be seen as odd. The reason being is because a bank is simply there to hold onto money so that you can either spend it in paper form or digital form. The rest of a bank's job is validation. You have to validate that you have the money in the account, you have to validate that you have the ability to take out that loan, you have to validate almost everything you do with a bank account but with Ethereum it is automatically validated.

Therefore, if it isn't illegal now, banks will attempt to lobby to get it to be illegal because they would literally die as a business if it became the standard.

Why Ethereum won't be the Last Altcoin

The reason why there are many alternative cryptocurrency coins in the first place is because people found better ways to do stuff. This won't be the first and won't be the last, well I know it obviously won't be the first but it will not definitely be the last. If there is anything to learn from the current alternative cryptocurrencies out there and the top dog of them all right now, which is Bitcoin, people just keep on creating different cryptocurrencies simply because they want to make the best one that everybody wants to invest in and this means that until someone comes on top with all the neat features and little gadgets that we want, there will never be a last alternative currency.

Chapter 6: Storing Ethereum Coins

Hard Storage

Just like Bitcoin, there are a few ways to store Ethereum coins and the truth of the matter is that there are really only three ways to store these alternative coins. The first, primary method, is to store the coin on a more permanent type of platform. The first method of hard storage is to simply store it on the hard drive that you do your mining and you're investing on, which is what most beginners begin to store their hard earned Ethereum coins on so that it's just the easiest method possible. For this, you're handed a digital wallet that can keep track of those coins along with any other transactions that you might have had on the same network.

The more security-conscious individuals that have gathered quite a bit more Ethereum coins often try to store these coins on medium storages such as a USB stick or an SD card. The reason why this is more security conscious is because a USB stick or an SD card can be hidden throughout the house without being attached to a very big and identifying computer source. This means that it's much harder to steal the USB stick or SD card in this case but the added bonus is that if your computer gets infected with a ransomware virus or any type of key logger, the individual will only ever have access to those digital keys to the coins if they happen to have the virus on at the same time that you plug the device into the computer rather than 24 hours of the day. This is if you haven't been able to figure out where their virus is and haven't removed it from your computer because at this level, these things become more prominent to your view and so you keep up with the maintenance on your computer so as to keep it safe. The most popular and recommended cryptocurrency USB hard drive is the Ledger Nano S.

For more information about the Ledger Nano S Hard wallet, visit wonpublications.com/ledger

There are a few problems with these types of storage mediums because these types of storage mediums are known for being somewhat volatile by nature. If you whack a USB against a hard surface for a very long time there is a very high chance that all of the data is completely wiped from the USB stick or the data becomes corrupt and this is the truth of the SD card as well because these two platforms are very volatile. A less volatile platform would be that of an Solid State Storage Drive, otherwise known as an SSD. This type of Drive is very durable and very quick whenever writing information to it so you wouldn't need to keep it connected to the computer for very long but they are significantly more expensive than their counterparts of storage. There is also the potential that you can lose your hard wallet. Most people keep their USB's on their house keychains or car keychains for protection, but in the chance you lose it, it's impossible to get the data back.

Paper Storage

The second method of storing your Ethereum coins is to simply create a paper that controls all of the digits that you have and this is normally referred to as the paper money of cryptocurrency. The reason why paper money is utilize is because not only is it very difficult to grab all the keys at once, unlike the digital platforms of both the USB stick or the SSD but it is also rather difficult to physically steal all of your paper notes. For example, you don't need all of your paper notes should you leave the house and so a person who doesn't understand cryptocurrency would not understand the value behind a stack of papers with random digits on it. Imagine if you were a burglar and you had no idea of cryptocurrency and so when you saw that a victim had a stack of pieces of paper with ciphers on them, what exactly would you think at that point? This form of currency is widely used by the heavily secure conscious people but it does come with the added problem of having to manually enter any of the keys that you stored on paper. This means that transactions could take considerably longer than they would normally take if you had a digital wallet and you would have to wipe your drive free of the coins on your account in order for the paper money to actually mean anything. Needless to say, this is really only utilized by individuals who intend to take their paper money with them to a specific spot where they are going to hand over the bill of cryptocurrency to a vendor or they simply want to be more security conscious of their money.

Cloud Storage

Cloud storage is the third and final form of storing your Ethereum coins and this refers to either having a website where you store your Ethereum coins like you would on a regular hard drive or where it is an online wallet that allows you to do transactions. There are risks with either of these options. With a cloud storage medium, you run into the risk of anyone gaining access to the password of your cloud storage device or if the cloud storage service itself becomes a target of being hacked where all the information of the customers are stolen. Additionally, with both of the services you run into the risk of an employee having access to your account and seeing a giant amount of Ethereum coins being stored on your cloud storage. If they were very good at what they did in their IT job then they could simply steal the coins and make it look like it was never there in the first place. The problem with an online wallet is that there are no real trusted organizations at this point that will hold your Ethereum coins in an online wallet and so you run into the risk where if you want to do this method, you need to understand that the owner of this wallet could easily just take all the coins that you saved up inside of that wallet. This has actually happened more than once and many people have lost thousands of cryptocurrency due to these shady individuals. In fact, these shady individuals are generally the reason why most people simply don't even look out the cloud storage possibility of storing their cryptocurrency. Having said that, cloud storage is also the easiest form of storing these digital forms of cryptocurrency because you can generally access these drives from anywhere that you wanted to such as inside of a crypto-currency bar or on the streets with your cell phone plan. Needless to say, a lot of people like to store small bits of their cryptocurrency on their online drives so as to have immediate access to it if they want to buy something in their cryptocurrency.

There are many pros and cons to all types of storages. Personally I'm not a big user of hard wallets, but I know some individuals love and are reliable with hard ware devices. An alternative method would be diversifying all of these. I know some people like to have some on their Ledger Nano S and some on an online wallet. It is completely up to you.

Chapter 7: Trading in Ethereum

Paper for Digital

The first thing that you can do with a cryptocurrency is actually switch it from a cryptocurrency back to the Fiat money that is more usable in Daily applications. Most people think that these applications for cryptocurrency are very small and very dense so they don't want to fully invest into the cryptocurrency market but rather get the rewards from the cryptocurrency market that they would receive if they turned their hard-earned cryptocurrency into cash. For instance, if you manage to grab a Bitcoin for the day then you would easily have thousands of dollars because Bitcoins are currently worth thousands of dollars per Bitcoin. However, the common use for the cryptocurrency is to just let it save up and then once it becomes something that you can utilize, you either go through a digital currency exchange like BitPay, where you can change your Bitcoins or your alternative coins into actual Fiat money. This is a very flexible way to work with the money but at the same time there are some issues that come up with the worth of a Bitcoin if you are too slow to do this or you are too quick to do this.

Digital for Digital

A less common trend amongst the average individual who just does mining for cryptocurrency for fun, but an equally common trend amongst investors who treat cryptocurrency like it's a stock trade is the fact that you can trade cryptocurrency for cryptocurrency. Therefore, if you earn a certain portion of Ethereum as it is right now and then trade that Ethereum for Ethereum Classic because you might think it will do better then you can go on to a market for that and trade for cryptocurrencies. The idea behind this is that certain cryptocurrencies rise in value faster than others and so what ends up happening is that people want to earn a cryptocurrency that's popular right now but also want to trade it for something that they think is on the rise and will rise quicker than the one they are earning. This may not make sense for a lot of people but the honest truth about it is that if you have something that's worth more value than the item that you want but the item that you want is going to have more value in the future, then it makes sense to not spend time working on the one that you want if it is easier to work on the one that you have. This is the concept of trading digital currency with other digital currency.

Performing Work for Ethereum

As odd as it may seem, many people are willing to work for alternate cryptocurrencies because of the worth of the cryptocurrency at the time. In fact, there are websites that are specifically dedicated to offering job positions based off of Bitcoin. Even a company like Fiverr has joined the mix by offering an option to pay out in Bitcoin. This is because Bitcoin removes the barriers Because alternate current cryptocurrencies are based on the Bitcoin model, they also happen to remove the barrier to many of the problems that come with Fiat money. Fiat money has to go through a middleman, which we all know as a bank, but Banks often come with transaction fees, wire transfer fees, and foreign or national fees that end up piling on top of other fees to make the transaction almost a nightmare for anything that is of a small size. If you are just trying to switch over a currency for a few hundred dollars then you don't want to pay nearly $60 in fees just so that you can do that and so these alternate cryptocurrencies allow you to make that exchange. Additionally, most of the time you can just trade in your Bitcoin or your alternate currency into a system like BitPay where you deposit the amount of money that you want with a fee from BitPay for doing the service for you into your account directly rather than trying to use the bank's system of converting money. A good example of why I would use Bitcoin is if I were to have another customer from Australia because when I got paid through PayPal with Australian money, the exchange rate was absolutely horrible and I actually lost $60 on a $300 invoice. That is nearly one-fifth of the money that I made that went into a conversion fee just because PayPal needed that money to correct the value difference between the two currencies. I would go through a service like BitPay where I might pay a 5% or 10% fee in an exchange so that I can change that Australian dollars into United States dollars. This is actually one of the most common practices for an application inside of the cryptocurrency environment but it's not the only form of work that can be paid with cryptocurrency. The other form of work is actually at convenience stores or restaurants because there are locations that are specifically designed so that they can accept Bitcoin as payment. In these places you use Bitcoin as regular money and you simply just hand them your address where they transfer the necessary amount of Bitcoins from your address and to their address. This makes the process of having to deal with any Fiat money virtually non-existent and some owners of buildings actually accept a form of currency in the cryptocurrency market because they know that the value of that cryptocurrency is likely to go up so they see it as a loss for the person who is spending the money but also a gain on their part because whenever they accept the cryptocurrency they will be accepting a currency that will likely rise in value and so it will be worth more than it was originally when they accepted it.

Chapter 8: Ethereum as a Trade Market

Buy High Sell Short

There are four main ways to trade in side of the Ethereum Market and this really depends on what you want to do with it. You have to remember that the market for Ethereum is very similar to the trade market and so when you hear these terms, which are the titles of these paragraphs, they will be almost identical to the terms that are utilized inside of stock trading. Therefore, when you buy high and sell short, what it means is that you are waiting for the moment when the Ethereum looks like it's going to be worth less than what it's going to be worth in just 5 to 20 minutes down the road. Essentially, the idea is that if you manage to buy at a certain time, you can make a little bit of money back by waiting until the value of the product rises and this is actually generally how stock trade marketing is done in the first place the only difference is that this is Ethereum and cryptocurrencies are actually well known to be rather volatile so buying high and selling short is one of the most common practices when it comes to trading the product that is Ethereum.

Buy Low Sell Short

Now buying low and selling short is a lot less common due to the fact that Ethereum is rarely ever at a low point in the market. There are crashes in Ethereum and there are small Pockets where Ethereum might lose some value but the idea is that if you see the product losing value for maybe $0.20 for every single Ethereum going, you then buy because you know that there is going to be a rise because there's usually a rise. Performed in succession, you can usually come out on top by buying low and waiting a short bit for the price to come back up but you run the risk of buying during the time that a cryptocurrency is currently having a crash. The problem with this is that you spend a lot of money to buy these coins in the first place. Ethereum is approximately $300 in monetary USD value as of writing this book, and if I were to go and buy five of these coins, they would be the equivalent of $1,500 but if the market for Ethereum were to suddenly crash then I would have the problem of waiting until the price for Ethereum went back up over $1,500 before I ever made any money. Some people panic at this point because they believe that this Ethereum might not go back up but the proof is in the pudding that the cryptocurrencies usually go back up. These people panic and sell too early and wind up losing a little bit of money just so that they can stay safe and only lose a little bit of money. If the Ethereum doesn't come back up then they've lost that money and usually, when you're buying something like stocks, you don't buy in small quantities.

Buy Low Sell Long

Now this brings us to the other type of trade marketing and that is to simply buy it when it's low and wait a long time before you sell it. This actually makes sense for a lot of the alternative currencies because they've almost always started off slow and then a few years later they're at monstrously high peaks in terms of monetary value. Many of the individuals who may have amassed nearly a thousand Bitcoins cashed out once Bitcoin hit a certain thousand-dollar point. Well, if you have a thousand bitcoins that are worth a couple thousand dollars, you then have, basically, a million to 2 million dollars. This is the long game and it is considered the unwise decision when it comes to any type of stock trading at all. Most people prefer to sell short because it is easier to predict the market if you look at the market in small pictures rather than in very long strides. Usually, the only people who actually sell like this are individuals who are absolute fanatics at whatever they're buying.

Mine and Exchange

The last part of the stock exchange for Ethereum is to actually just feed the market because if you are a miner and you can produce the amount of Ethereum that you need to, you don't have to worry about the buying price of Ethereum until it falls. Most of your worrying, as a miner, is how much is the coin worth in terms of the voltage that you're utilizing in order to mine the coins. This final form is what ultimately drives the stock trade market for Ethereum because it introduces new coins into the mixture and creates the fluctuations of values that you see in the market that many of these players of the Ethereum Market play off of.

I've been investing for years and it's something I am truly passionate about. Since I started investing in cryptocurrencies, I've learnt a lot. I know as a beginner it can be extremely confusing, that's is why I dedicated my time to this series. If you're enjoying this book, please leave a review on Amazon.

For a FREE course on how to buy your first Bitcoin, Litecoin, and Ethereum,

Get $10 worth of Bitcoin for free when you register today and invest $100

Visit wonpublications.com/crypto

Chapter 9: Mining Ethereum

What is CPU and GPU Mining?

To begin with the history of currency cryptocurrency mining, we first have to start with the CPU and this is because the CPU is where people first started figuring out how to solve these different blockchains. With most of the cryptocurrency mining that you do on a daily basis, you will still have access to CPU and GPU mining but certain pools are preventing the use of CPUs and GPUs. Essentially, the CPU would get a blockchain that it needed to figure out and this was okay because the CPU might have had a certain amount of cores but almost all of those cores usually ran anywhere from 2.5 to 4.0 gigahertz. This was when you started seeing a huge mountain of people purchasing CPU cores that were meant for servers because servers would be able to provide you with anywhere from 12 to 16 cores running at around 3 to 4 gigahertz. This was mind-blowingly fast at the time but the problem is that everything gets harder as more people get interested into cryptocurrency.

You can see why the industry of cryptocurrency switched from the CPU to the GPU. You see, the GPU is a fantastic little device if you can figure out how to use it because it is built for simple calculations and it has thousands of smaller cores that run in succession or parallel. These smaller cores allowed individuals to replicate the act of mining but at an explosively rapid rate. This has actually been the tradition for the past few years because people keep on buying the newest GPU on the market but the problem is that the GPU market wasn't quite ready for the influx of cryptocurrency miners and so this market has only really been dealing with gaming computers when it comes to these high-end GPUs. They don't mass produce these GPUs on a level that the mining Community would purchase them at. For instance, one mining warehouse that is specifically dedicated to mining cryptocurrency will usually by anywhere from 300 to 400 GPUs. Now imagine that there are over four hundred companies buying GPUs in this amount and more. Needless to say, whenever a new GPU would hit the market, the market would essentially become devoid of that GPU because of the cryptocurrency miners. This has been the problem for the past year or so and so even though you can still utilize your CPU and GPU, don't expect to make the big bucks like you could have if you had invested in this around two to three years ago. Around that time, the hashes weren't that complex and the actual value of the coins were reasonable to the point where people were getting into the game just because they wanted to get into the game not because each coin represented thousands of dollars. Now that each coin represents thousands of dollars, everyone wants the new type of device that is specifically dedicated to cryptocurrency mining and this device allows individuals to go from the previous mega hashes that they used to experience with at least one GPU to a gigahash per device. We'll talk about why these different hash sizes are important in a little bit.

ASIC Mining

ASIC is the new device when it comes to cryptocurrency mining and it stands for Application-specific integrated-circuit. Therefore, it is specifically meant to perform cryptocurrency mining and this device usually costs the same amount of money that you would actually spend on a computer and that's because this is a very specialized device. These devices are extremely difficult to make for the public but they have almost always existed. In fact, Cisco is a proud owner of many of these types of devices but these devices that are coming out with cryptocurrency versions are not the same as the ones that Cisco provides. These devices are specifically built to only be used for the big bad boy otherwise known as Bitcoin mining. Due to this fact, many of the alternative coins are still utilizing CPU and GPU miners. Additionally, due to the fact that Bitcoin is so difficult to make money on without this device, many people are mining alternative coins in an attempt to actually make any money off of it.

Understanding The Market

The first thing that I have to cover is what the difference between a megahash and a gigahash. A megahash refers to how many megabytes can be transferred from the hash set in the blockchain and gigahash represents it in gigabytes. The faster that these two are the more money you can make but don't be fooled into thinking that you can just take your average GPU or CPU and generate some money off of it because there are a few things that you need to understand about the cost and benefit analysis before you even think that you're ready.

The first thing that you need to understand is the loss or rather the cost of electricity because that is the primary bill that you are going to be paying while trying to mine for the stuff. If you cannot cryptocurrency mine faster than your device causes electricity to be withdrawn then you are actually losing money and not making any money, which is why most people hit the newest GPUs on the market simply because those GPU cores are capable of providing the big hashset numbers that you need to make money while also doing it at a relatively low wattage amount. This allows individuals to build big gaming engines for computers and turns them into mining computers whenever they're out and about but they don't actually lose out because they process faster than they use electricity.

The other thing you need to pay attention to because the value of the coin really determines whether the benefit-cost analysis of your electricity in your house set really even matters. If your coin is super difficult to gather hash sets on then you are likely not going to make any money off of it. This is because the harder it is to gain hash sets the less money that your GPU or CPU is going to generate. If your coin doesn't actually represent a worth that represents its difficulty, then there is no sense in mining for it. Let's take my graphics card, which is an R9 270x. This is actually a graphics card that's really cheap and good for gaming. I haven't had to replace it ever since I bought it two years ago while it was Black Friday. I can still run some of the newest games in 60fps at 1080p because I just don't care about 4K.

Having said that, my graphics card runs at about 8.9 megahashes. Now my electricity costs around $0.07 per thousands of watts per hour (KW/hr). Now, if you think that's impressive then you should sit back and wonder why I have such a graphics card because that graphics card would earn me a total of $4 a month. That's right, a graphics card that is capable of running some of the newest games at 60fps at 1080p will only earn me $4 a month while mining for Ethereum. This is because my graphics card is built for handling DirectX 11 based games and not the newest form of DirectX or even the Vulcan architecture that was recently developed by AMD. Therefore, while my graphics card is impressive, that doesn't mean squat in the cryptocurrency world because unless I have a very high core amount along with some very high processing amount, my graphics card is one of the weakest ones out there. That's not to say anything bad about my graphics card though because if you look at the new version of AMD Vega, which is a graphics card that costs nearly $500, it actually runs at about 40 megahashes. That is an improvement but it's nowhere near the amount that would justify running this thing 24/7 for an entire month because the estimated worth of what I would make off of that is just 45 bucks. Needless to say, you are going to need something like a GPU mining rig where you have close to ten to twenty of these AMD Vegas so that you can make any worthwhile money off of it.

The Ethereum Wallet

Now, something that's not really mentioned the whole lot in beginning cryptocurrency tutorials is that you need to have a wallet and that wallet is not well described. I'm going to break it down really simple for you so that you understand no matter how technically advanced you maybe. A wallet is just a software that keeps track of the specific hash algorithms you managed to solve in a network along with your username attached to it. It just keeps track of a long list of different encrypted text and that's it. Therefore, when they talk about a wallet in cryptocurrency what they are talking about is a software that keeps a long list of encrypted text in a text file with a very nice graphical user interface to make it easier to work with. Now my preferred wallet is actually Exodus because Exodus allows you to create multiple different wallets for multiple different currencies and if you are into farming a certain currency one day or a certain currency the next month. It doesn't matter, it will create a currency wallet for you and it's extremely easy to use.

Mining in Pools

The other part about this is that you will never be mining solo because you likely do not have the power to do this. Unless you are a millionaire or a billionaire reading this book, you are likely never going to have the power to solo mine or rather solar mine and outperform a pool mine. A pool mine or when people get together in a group and mine a specific part of the network means that all the CPU, GPU, and devices are coupled into one giant massive CPU that calculates the hash. This means that if the person in the pool has a GPU that can run a megahash at about 8.9 like I can and then there's also another person that can run a terrahash at about 10, then the person with the terahash is obviously going to solve the problem first but because I'm in the pool, I get to benefit from them solving the problem. It results in a much smaller portion of the coin that is released onto the market because the coin is split amongst everyone in a pool but at least I get some portion of the coin for the effort that I allowed my computer to take inside of figuring out the hatch. Therefore, it's almost always better to mine in pools rather than solo mine.

Getting Connected

So the first thing that you're going to want to do is download the wallet that I mentioned before because this is how I'm going to run this tutorial. Once you install this, you will be given an option to choose which coin you want to create a wallet for. After you create this wallet, you will have a right-hand menu where you can select additional wallets that you want to create. Whenever you create this wallet, it will generate an automatic wallet hash algorithm that you can then use as your identifying marker. This is normally placed below the receive and send button and above the calculated amount of coins you have of that currency. This will be known as your *whatever* currency address. Once you have downloaded that, you can then actually go to a website known as nanopool.org. This website has a long list of different alternative coins that you can mine utilizing the wallet that I just mentioned. Pick a currency version that you want to utilize and then click on the quick start button. Once you have clicked on the quick start button, you can receive a lot of useful information that you will not understand until you've been into cryptocurrency for a long time but the important part is that at the bottom of the page it will tell you how to actually connect to the mining resource for that cryptocurrency. Now this is the part that they don't tell you. Let's go ahead and cover how you would connect your mining resource once you've downloaded the Claymore DualMiner that is suggested on the website. So what you're downloading is a ZIP file and you're going to want to extract these files into a singular folder so that there are easy to locate. Once you've extracted them, you want to look through and you are either going to be editing a bat file or you are going to be editing a config file. For Ethereum, we are going to edit a bat file. You will recognize the file as start_only_eth.bat, which is something that you're going to right click on and click edit. This will open up notepad where you can then edit the information inside of the bat file. The bat file represents a command line executable so when you double click on it, it will run in the command line, which is something that you will need to tackle with your antivirus or your firewall. You are essentially looking for this line:

EthDcrMiner64.exe -epool eth-eu1.nanopool.org:9999 -ewal address/worker/email -epsw x -mode 1 -ftime 10

Now if you remember correctly, I told you where the address was for your wallet and where you see the address area after ewall, you will need to paste in the address to your wallet there. Then you will need to erase the worker default and apply your own name(what you feel like calling it). The final parameter is an option and you don't actually have to utilize it but it allows you to know when your worker is on or offline. Once you have edited this, you can then save it and close the notepad. Then you can double-click on the bat file and watch it go. Once it gets started up, it will tell you how fast it is figuring out the hatches and it will tell you how fast your hash rate is. From there you can actually determine whether your PC is capable of providing you with any money or not off of this venture. If not but if you want to continue it further, you're going to have to buy better GPUs because the current ASIC devices are primarily designed for Bitcoin only.

Conclusion

Congratulations! Welcome to the end of this book! You're now an expert in Ethereum, and while this may be the end of this book, this is definitely not likely going to be all that you learn about Ethereum. Vitalik Buterin is constantly working on expanding the Ethereum network and out of all the cryptocurrencies, Ethereum contains the largest potential. You can see this on the market, being the second largest cryptocurrency after Bitcoin. Keep your eyes on Ethereum, it is the one to watch in the upcoming years, and I personally am a true believer in the project.

I hope you received valuable from this book, if you enjoyed this book, please leave a review on Amazon.com. Any review is greatly appreciated and I would like to thank you again for choosing this book. I strive to do the best I can and constantly revise the content.

www.ingramcontent.com/pod-product-compliance
Lightning Source LLC
Chambersburg PA
CBHW071237220526
45468CB00002B/892